Rachel Carson

by Emily James

CAPSTONE PRESS
a capstone imprint

Pebble Plus is published by Capstone Press,
1710 Roe Crest Drive, North Mankato, Minnesota 56003
www.mycapstone.com

Library of Congress Cataloging-in-Publication Data
Names: James, Emily, 1983– , author.
Title: Rachel Carson / by Emily James.
Description: North Mankato, Minnesota : Capstone Press, 2017. | Series:
Pebble plus. Great scientists and inventors | Includes bibliographical references and index. |
Audience: Ages 4 to 8. | Audience: Grades K to 3.
Identifiers: LCCN 2016023235|
ISBN 9781515738817 (library binding) | ISBN 9781515738879 (pbk.) |
ISBN 9781515739050 (ebook (pdf)
Subjects: LCSH: Carson, Rachel, 1907–1964—Juvenile literature. |
Biologists—United States—Biography—Juvenile literature. |
Environmentalists—United States—Biography—Juvenile literature. |
Science writers—United States—Biography—Juvenile literature.
Classification: LCC QH31.C33 J36 2017 | DDC 570.92 [B] —dc23
LC record available at https://lccn.loc.gov/2016023235

Editorial Credits
Jaclyn Jaycox and Michelle Hasselius, editors; Jennifer Bergstrom, designer;
Jo Miller, media researcher; Steve Walker, production specialist

Photo Credits
Alamy: B Christopher, 19, Victor de Schwanberg, 15; Corbis via Getty Images: George
Rinhart, 13; Getty Images: Archive Photos/JHU Sheridan Libraries/Gado, 5, The LIFE Picture
Collection/Alfred Eisenstaedt, 7, 21, The LIFE Picture Collection/Hank Walker, 11; Newscom:
Everett Collection, cover, 1, 9, 17
Design Elements: Shutterstock: aliraspberry, Charts and BG, mangpor2004, Ron and Joe,
sumkinn, Yurii Andreichyn

Note to Parents and Teachers

The Great Scientists and Inventors set supports national curriculum standards for
social studies related to people, places, and culture. This book describes and illustrates
the life of Rachel Carson. The images support early readers in understanding the text.
The repetition of words and phrases helps early readers learn new words. This book
also introduces early readers to subject-specific vocabulary words, which are defined
in the Glossary section. Early readers may need assistance to read some words and to
use the Table of Contents, Glossary, Read More, Internet Sites, Critical Thinking Using
the Common Core, and Index sections of the book.

Printed and bound in China.

PO7886LEOS17

Table of Contents

EARLY LIFE

Famous scientist and
environmentalist Rachel Carson
was born in 1907. She grew
up on a farm in Pennsylvania.
Rachel loved to read and write.

Rachel at age 26

Rachel's mother took Rachel on nature walks. Rachel learned about animals, birds, and flowers. She was happiest when she was in nature.

Rachel enjoyed nature throughout her life.

EARLY WORK

Rachel went to college. She earned degrees in biology and zoology. In 1936 she started working as a marine biologist at the U.S. Bureau of Fisheries.

Rachel in 1944

Rachel wrote articles for
newspapers and magazines.
She wrote three books
about the ocean. The books
made Rachel famous.

Rachel in 1952

FINDING THE TRUTH

In 1958 Rachel began studying a pesticide called DDT. It was used to kill insects. But DDT was also harmful to plants, animals, and even people.

Rachel wrote a book in 1962 called *Silent Spring*. It was about the bad effects of DDT. Many people didn't believe her. But studies proved she was right.

By the same Author

•

UNDER THE SEA-WIND
THE SEA AROUND US
THE EDGE OF THE SEA

SILENT SPRING

BY

RACHEL CARSON

Introduction by
LORD SHACKLETON

Preface by
SIR JULIAN HUXLEY, F.R.S.

HAMISH HAMILTON
LONDON

Rachel became very sick. But she wanted to get her message out. She spoke on TV and to the government about pesticides. Rachel died in 1964.

Rachel spoke to the government about pesticides on January 4, 1963.

Rachel's work helped start the environmental movement. In 1970 the U.S. government created the Environmental Protection Agency (EPA). The EPA banned DDT in 1972.

The United States EPA headquarters in Washington, D.C.

In 1980 Rachel was given the Presidential Medal of Freedom for her work. She changed the way people treat the environment.

Glossary

biology—the study of plant and animal life

bureau—an office that provides information or some other service

college—a school that students attend after high school

degree—a title given to a person for finishing a course of study in college

environment—all of the trees, plants, water, and dirt

environmentalist—a person who works to protect wildlife and natural areas

insect—a small animal with a hard outer shell, six legs, three body sections, and two antennae; most insects have wings

marine biologist—a scientist who studies plants and animals that live in the ocean

pesticide—a chemical used to kill pests, such as insects

Presidential Medal of Freedom—the highest honor someone outside of the military can receive from the U.S. government

zoology—the science of studying animals

Read More

Hile, Lori. *Rachel Carson: Environmental Pioneer.* Women in Conservation. Chicago: Heinemann Library, 2015.

Hustad, Douglas. *Environmentalist Rachel Carson.* STEM Trailblazer Bios. Minneapolis: Lerner Publications, 2016.

Lawlor, Laurie. *Rachel Carson and Her Book That Changed the World.* New York: Holiday House, 2012.

Internet Sites

FactHound offers a safe, fun way to find Internet sites related to this book. All of the sites on FactHound have been researched by our staff.

Here's all you do:

Visit *www.facthound.com*

Type in this code: 9781515738817

Super-cool stuff! Check out projects, games and lots more at **www.capstonekids.com**

Critical Thinking Using the Common Core

1. Rachel was an environmentalist. What do environmentalists do? (Craft and Structure)

2. Rachel wrote a book called *Silent Spring*. What was the book about? (Key Ideas and Details)

3. Describe two ways Rachel spoke out about pesticides. (Key Ideas and Details)

Index